The Florence

An Era of Elegance

COLLECTIBLES

Doug Foland

Schiffer Publishing Ltd

77 Lower Valley Road, Atglen, PA 19310

DEDICATION

For my beloved family, whom I love very much.

To Florence Ward. In your tragedy, you chose to create beautiful works of art. They have brought me and others countless hours of joy.

To all Florence collectors. May you enjoy the search as much as I have.

For Sister Maria Francls and her staff of Out Reach Ministry in Portland, Oregon, for their years of tireless service to the poor and forgotten.

To the Outside In staff in Portland for their work with the homeless and their AIDS Education Program.

The two above-mentioned charities will share fifty percent of the royalties from this book.

Library of Congress Cataloging-in Publication Data

Foland, Doug.
The Florence collectibles : an era of elegance : with value guide /
Doug Foland.
p. cm. – (A Schiffer Book for collectors)
ISBN 0-88740-870-2
1. Ward, Florence–Catalogs. 2. Florence Ceramics Company–Catalogs. 3.
Pottery figures–California–Pasadena–Catalogs. 4. Pottery–20th century–
California–Pasadena–Catalogs.
I. Title. II. Series.
NK4210.W26A4   1995
738.8'2'0979493075–dc20   95-24294
CIP

Printed in Hong Kong
ISBN: 0-88740-870-2

We are interested in hearing from authors with book ideas on related subjects.

Published by
Schiffer Publishing Ltd.
77 Lower Valley Road
Atglen, PA 19310

Please write for a free catalog.
This book may be purchased from the publisher.
Please include $2.95 for shipping.
Try your bookstore first

ACKNOWLEDGMENTS

SPECIAL THANKS

There are three reasons why I was able to complete the lengthy task of researching and writing this book. First is my love for Florence ceramics; second is my admiration for the work being done by the two Portland charities to which I have assigned 50% of my royalties; and third is the help of Lisbeth Brody.

I would like to thank Lisbeth for her encouragement when I first got the idea of writing this book and for her technical support in getting my ideas onto the page. She is a friend, former English teacher, and computer person without whom I could not have gotten beyond second base—I did not even know what the computer term "user friendly" meant. She has been a blessing to me and has given her time for the good of others. May she be blessed in all she does throughout her life.

A very special thanks to Jeannie Fredericks, whom I met a year and a half ago over the telephone. Jeannie has unstintingly shared her expertise and knowledge in identifying, pricing, researching, and generally encouraging. She kindly allowed us to invade her home and photograph her beautiful collection. I could not have done it without her.

There are countless family members, friends, collectors, dealers, and many others who have helped me in so many ways. You know who you are—I send my heartfelt thanks! Special thanks to my sister, Sue, for her patience and support driving the L.A. freeways, and to my mother, brothers, and their families for their encouragement.

Thanks go to:

Betty Carson, a long-time dealer and collector, for her encouragement and years of knowledge.

Jack Chipman, author of *California Pottery,* for his help in providing copyright marks of the Florence collection;

Ruby Clancy for sharing her memories of the four years she worked for the Florence Company;

Janet Cudar and her sister for sharing their vast pool of information;

Yolanda De LaCruz for her many efforts, including hours spent searching through catalogues for names, prices and colors;

Louise and Glen Everett for driving several hours to Portland to allow us to photograph over 100 pieces which would not otherwise have been included in the book;

Judith Ford for her support, encouragement and countless hours spent researching and writing;

Jerry and Sue Kline, owners of The Past Time Collectible in Gatlinburg, Tennessee, for the wealth of information, sage advice on pricing, and the lovely photos of their collection;

Ron Lindsay and his wife for their encouragement, for sharing a great many facts, and for their assistance with pricing for the Southwest;

Dave and Penny Miller for their encouragement and willingness to provide the names of countless figurines of which I was not aware;

Don Pine for his keen eye in searching the negatives and pictures, and for his support and encouragement;

Dave and Penny Renner for their valuable information;

Dennis Scott, of Dennis Massachusetts Antiques, for his help with the New England pricing;

Patti and Dave Smith for their hospitality when they invited us to their home to photograph their collection, and for the information they were willing to share;

Don Springer for his hours of proof-reading, minute checking of facts, and following to the finish with every detail;

Clifford Ward, Jr., for his time, interest, and assistance in bringing to this book information which might otherwise have gone unknown.

PHOTOGRAPHIC CREDITS

I would like to acknowledge the following people for their wonderful work in photographing all of the pieces which appear in this book. My thanks to each of you - I could not have done it without you.

Carlos Sayan, Pasadena, California;

Ron Anicker, Portland, Oregon; and

Jerry Kline, Gatlinburg, Tennessee.

FOREWORD

My first experience with Florence ceramics was at age 16, when I visited my Aunt Zella in Hastings, Nebraska. She had a large, grand house with countless treasures everywhere. Zella and her husband had been in the jewelry business. They had a lovely store filled with not only jewelry, but also Florence figurines and artware from the Florence line of ceramics.

I remember admiring the ladies on the settees and being especially drawn to the Story Hour group. I remember Zella commenting that she thought Florence was the first to use real lace in her pieces. The lace was applied to the actual piece before firing, with elegant results. It gave a truly grand effect. My aunt also told me that the articulated fingers of the Florence pieces were some of the first in this country.

Now, at 43, I have found over 40 figurines during the course of my life and travels. They are all large pieces and in mint condition. A great delight in writing this book has been my opportunity to meet others who share my love of the Florence work and see their lovely collections.

One of my main reasons for publishing this book was to show the true elegance of ceramics made in America. From other countries have come the ceramics of Hummel, Meissen, Dresden, Lladró, Royal Doulton, Limoges and others. We in the United States have been graced with Florence. It was my wish to honor the Ward family, which was able to face its hour of grief and turn it into work which has brought great joy to so many lives. It is my pleasure to offer this beautiful collection in a book which can bring enjoyment to others.

CONTENTS

Acknowledgements 3
Foreword 4

Chapter 1: The History of Florence Ceramics 6
Chapter 2: Prices of The 1940s & 1950s 9
Chapter 3: A Visit with Florence Ward's Family 11
Chapter 4: Collectors from Across the Country 15
Chapter 5: Early Garage Pieces 40
Chapter 6: Florence Pairs 46
Chapter 7: Godey Designs 58
Chapter 8: Children Figurines 66
Chapter 9: Figurine Flower Holders 80
Chapter 10: Artware 91
Chapter 11: Rare, Unusual, & Hard-To-Find Pieces 120
Chapter 12: An Array of Colors 131

Price Guides 142
   Price Guide for Named Figurines 142
   Unnamed Pieces 143
   Price Guide for Artware 143
   Figurine Size and Color Chart 144

CHAPTER 1
THE HISTORY OF FLORENCE CERAMICS

The year 1939 marked a vast array of events. In Europe, there were horrible atrocities taking place as Hitler's war progressed. New York was hosting a World's Fair to the delight of fairgoers. In southern California, tragedy struck the Ward family when they lost their youngest son to a streptococcus infection, at a time before antibiotic treatments were known.

For the first few years after the death of her son, friends urged Florence Ward to take up a hobby to help her move past her grief. Florence decided to take up modeling clay figurines in the family garage.

Florence bought her first kiln for $50.00. Because city codes might have been violated if she set up the kiln on the property where her house sat, the kiln was located nearby at a badminton court which was not being used in those war years. Many of her early pieces created here were of children. Compared to the elegance of her later work, these early pieces now seem somewhat crude. Several held the smile of her little boy, who had been called away in his childhood to an untimely death.

At the same time, Florence's husband Clifford was working for the war department as a contractor in Salt Lake City, Utah. Her firstborn son, Clifford Ward, Jr., was a U.S. Marine dive-bomber pilot flying missions in the South Pacific.

When Florence first displayed her early works from her garage at 1644 North Lake Avenue in Pasadena, her friends and neighbors were amazed. They urged her to market her lovely pieces. Word spread of her exquisite skill and she received her first order for 84 pieces. Deciding this was a wonderful opportunity to take her clay beyond a hobby, she conceived the idea that she would build a business. This business would be there for her husband and son when they returned from the war. According to Clifford Ward, Jr., he and his father were totally surprised when they returned home. They had no idea Florence had these previously unknown, natural artistic talents, nor that she had used her gift to start such a dynamic business.

The Florence Ceramics Company operated in two smaller facilities before moving to the final plant in 1948. Florence, Clifford Sr. and Clifford Jr. occupied a 13,000 square foot plant with one entire wall made of glass to let in the sunlight. The spacious, well-designed plant had the newest equipment, including a tunnel kiln; but, more than merely a factory, it was an extension of Florence Ward the artist. It gave Florence pleasure to offer tours to the public each Wednesday at 1 p.m. as a way of sharing some of her excitement with the process.

Florence, her factory, employees, and figurines as they appeared in one of the original catalogues.

Florence was the sole designer of the semi-porcelain figurines, lamps, and artware. According to her son, Clifford Ward, Jr., "she was a natural when it came to her artistic creations." Florence chose to model her figurines from several periods of history. There were also characters from movies, and fictional characters inspired by plays she might have seen or books she had read. She delighted in children, something quite evident in the large number of children used in both the figurines and flower holders. The figurines Pamela and David are molded after her grandchildren, Clifford Ward, Jr.'s son and daughter. She made both "plain" and "fancy" versions for many of the figurines. A piece was considered plain when it was finished with a colored glaze only. Fancy pieces had added accessories such as hats, bows, flowers, purses, muffs, extra lace, 22K gold, etcetera.

Florence was annoyed by some of the religious figurines being produced to market at that time. She felt they were too futuristic. She spent a great deal of her time and energy researching the works of some of the great classical artists, including Raphael. With her wonderful talent, she was able to create beautiful religious pieces, like the Madonna and Child. She was certainly one of the first ceramic artists to create the mother and child as separate figurines. It was only after each figurine was completed that the two pieces were then placed together to make the Madonna and Child.

The Florence lamps were mounted on either hardwood or polished brass bases. These were made in three sizes. The 19.5" Scarlet lamp comes in green, rose, beige, and dubonnet (or egg shell) with a ruffled taffeta shade. On the 19.5" Camille lamp, the figurine is trimmed with matching lace and has a 12" round ninon shade. Other lamps included such figurines as Delia, Musette, Marie Antoinette, Claudia, Genevieve and Clarissa. The Elizabeth and Vivian are both 23.5". But the tallest and most expensive lamp was the 26.25" tall Madame Pompadour. This lamp was made in royal red, moss, and white.

The Florence Ceramics Company also made semi-porcelain clocks. These were painted china of assorted colors and were powered by electricity.

According to Clifford Ward, Jr., the brocade figurines were not as popular. They were also hard to work with and not as profitable because of the time it took to produce each one.

The Florence Collection was sold in finer department stores and jewelry stores. There were sales representatives and showrooms located throughout the United States, centered in Pasadena and San Francisco, California; Detroit, Michigan; Chicago, Illinois; Kansas City, Kansas; New York City, New York; and Dallas, Texas. The collection was also sold overseas. The largest sales overseas were in England. Beautiful ceramic dealer signs were given to the better retailers to set out on their glass counters which held the figurines. These dealer signs are rare and quite hard to find today.

The pieces in the Florence Collection were copyrighted at the time of creation. Many of the names of the pieces were actually written in the mold of the figurine. There were also many made unnamed. Below are several of the copyright stamps used at various times. The early pieces were signed in the molds or signed in gold paint by Florence.

I was delighted to be fortunate enough while finishing the research for this section of the book to be contacted by a former employee of the Florence Ceramics Company, Ruby Clancy. She is now retired in Portland, Oregon and called me after reading a newspaper story about the work I was doing to prepare this book.

Mrs. Clancy worked for Florence in the early 1950s for three or four years. She had previously worked at home. However, one of her children needed braces and it became necessary for her to find a way to pay for the braces. Since she lived only three blocks from the Florence Ceramics Company plant, she applied for a job. Though she did not have any production experience, she had a creative nature and had taken art classes in high school and college. She was hired and put to work on her first job in the Overglaze Decorating Room. This is where china paints and 22K gold were applied to the figurines and artware pieces and subsequently fired on the third trip through the kiln.

Nearby was the room where the pieces were airbrush-painted. This airbrush technique was started in 1951 at the Florence Ceramics Company. Before that time, the figurines were primarily gold and white with colored flowers, hats, parasols, muffs, etc.

Mrs. Clancy thought Florence and the whole Ward family were wonderful to work for. She remembers seeing Clifford Ward, Sr. working mostly in the room where the molds were poured and some other areas of the facility. She remembers Clifford Ward, Jr. at the plant daily, overseeing the operations. She described him as a quiet, thoughtful, and hardworking young man. She also remembers seeing Florence herself at the plant several times each week.

There was a ceramic engineer on staff whose area of responsibility was the paints and dyes. He evaluated the chemical reactions and other technical phases which would bring the colors from Florence's ideas onto the actual ceramic pieces. Other staff members included salesmen. However, the majority of the approximately 150 employees were the women who did the production work. They were paid on a piece rate basis. They usually earned two dollars or more per hour—a very good wage for that time.

Mrs. Clancy still has many warm memories of her years with the Florence Ceramics Company. She remembers how pleasant it was to work the eight hour shift in the plant because it was so modern and the Wards were so nice. The work required the employees to pay meticulous attention to detail, but this did not diminish the creativity required to do the job. At Christmas, the employees were all given gifts and a lovely party. Mrs. Clancy remembers that a few of the parties were actually at Florence's home in the foothills of Pasadena.

Mrs. Clancy's recollection from her years at the Florence Ceramics Company is that the Godey ladies were very strong sellers. Other pieces she remembers making in large numbers were Abigail, Matilda, and Melanie. She recalled conversations with several of her co-workers in which they all shared their belief that people several years into the future would be collecting the pieces then being made by the Florence Ceramics Company because the collection was so beautiful and of such high quality.

Though it has been forty years since Mrs. Clancy worked at Florence's plant, she remembers vividly the different rooms in the facility and the steps in the process of making the figurines.

1. The clay came from Kentucky, Tennessee, Florida and California. This clay was mixed with talc and feldspar to form a liquid slurry called slip. The slip was then poured into the molds. After a period of 30-45 minutes, the molds were carried over to drain. After an hour or two, the pieces could be removed from the molds. The pieces which were to be clay-decorated were put in special closets so they could be worked on the following day.

2. While the pieces were still damp, they were sent to the clay decorating room. (The employees nicknamed this room the "crud" room because the work with the wet clay was such a messy process.) The seams from the molding were sponged and worked until they were perfectly smooth. Any place on the figurine which bore any traces of the mold was also worked smooth. The quality control inspector checked each piece before it left this stage. The quality control standards were quite rigid. There was no variance allowed from the high standards of Florence. Any piece which was not absolutely perfect was sent back to the work station or discarded.

3. The arms and hands were made individually in their own tiny molds. In the clay decorating room, the different components of each piece were attached. The flowers, arms, hands, and all accessories were covered with a clay with the texture of whipped cream. This clay would help form the bond between the parts. They all had to be kept moist to allow the attached pieces to adhere smoothly, without showing any indication of the joining process.

4. One of the employees often worked at her home making the various flowers used on the pieces. These flowers were delivered daily to the plant. Real lace was dipped into a creamy clay, then fitted and gathered as it was pressed into the different areas of the figurine. This technique was developed by Florence, and gives her pieces an extraordinary beauty and exquisite detail found only in Florence ceramics.

5. The pieces were then fired in a tunnel kiln which stretched down one whole side of the factory. After the first firing, called a "bisque" firing, the pieces were dipped in glaze material and fired at over 1900 degrees Fahrenheit.

6. After the firing was completed, the pieces were sent to the Overglaze Decorating room. Here the fine detail such as the faces, gold trim or the words on the page of a book were added to the pieces. Following the overglaze decorating, the pieces received their decorating firing, at a lower temperature than the one previously used to melt and set the glazes.

7. Final quality inspections of each piece were made before any pieces were permitted to be sold.

Mrs. Clancy told me she would have liked to continue working at the Florence Ceramics Company, but she was expecting another child and felt she needed to focus her attention on being a full-time mother and home-maker. She and her family now live in the Pacific Northwest. She still has a nnumber of pieces which were pulled out as "seconds." I spent some time examining these "seconds." It is a testimony to the level of quality required by Florence that these pieces were not considered acceptable for sale, since I had a hard time finding any flaws. Many of the pieces Mrs. Clancy has in her collection bear her signature, as the plant artist. Some of her pieces are Dear Ruth, a mantle clock, Musette, Madame Pompadour, Louis XV, Victoria, and Elizabeth, as well as several compote and shell dishes.

One of the more difficult times faced at the Florence Ceramics Company was when the Lefton company began to pirate Florence's exquisite designs and turn out copies which they had produced using cheap overseas labor. Though the Florence Ceramics Company won two court battles over copyright infringement, The Lefton Company ultimately continued to make and import their cheap imitations by making slight alterations to Florence's design (see "Chapter 3: A Visit with the Family" for more information on this subject). This difficult period was followed by the death of Clifford Ward, Sr. in 1964. At this time, the Florence Ceramics Company production plant was sold to Scripto.

Scripto, however, did not acquire any of the copyrighted Florence figurine line. Scripto produced a new and very different line which included advertising mugs and commemorative plates. The Scripto company also produced two commemorative tankards. One was for the moon walk and one was for the astronauts' splashdown. The tankards bear the names of the astronauts, the July 20th date of the moon landing, as well as the following legend: "On July 20th, 1969, the National Aeronautics and Space Administration directed the first moon landing by man. Thus the United States of America became the first nation to complete a manned exploration of the lunar surface." After Scripto presented these tankards to Richard Nixon and Spiro Agnew, President Nixon ordered a hundred to be made with the Presidential Seal.

This unit of Scripto ceased to exist in 1977.

Florence's life did go on after her husband's death. As was so typical of her strength, she found the inner peace to later remarry. In 1991, at the age of 93, Florence died. She was survived by her son Clifford Ward, Jr., and his children, Pamela and David. Pamela continues to live in the Southern California area while David lives in Maine.

CHAPTER 2
PRICES OF THE 1940s and 1950s

Catalogs of the Florence collection were produced through 1957, and can be quite costly today (several purchased in 1969/1970 went for $100-$125). In the exciting time while I was researching this book, I was very fortunate to spend a day with Clifford Ward, Jr., who was kind enough to offer me some of the original catalogues from the 1950s. The following photos are from those catalogues.

Top Left Photo: A page from a 1954 catalogue; *Bottom Left Photo:* A page from a 1957 catalogue;

Center Right Photo: A page from a 1957 catalogue; *Center Right Photo:* A page from a 1951 catalogue;

Bottom Right Photo: A page from a 1951 catalogue.

You will notice that several of the finer pieces, such as Pinkie and Blue Boy, Story Hour, and Lillian Russell, were priced in the $30-50 range. In today's world, many people spend more than that each month buying their daily coffee from espresso vendors. However, in the early 1950s, there were many parts of the country where the typical working person spent $30-50 per month for the mortgage payment on the family home. It is a tribute to the elegance of Florence's creations and the quality of the work that people were eager to spend these sums on her newest pieces.

The following is a sampling of several pieces' original prices from the '40s and '50s.

Name of Piece	Original $	Name of Piece	Original $	Name of Piece	Original $
ABIGAIL	8	FALL	10	—ROSIE	3
AMBER	25	FERN	6	MIMI	3
AMELIA	8	GARY	10	MOLLY	3
ANN	4-6	GENEVIEVE	12	MUSETTE	17
ANNABEL	15	GEORGETTE	25	NANCY	5
AVA	8	GRACE	10	NELL GWEN	40
BARBARA	15	GRANDMOTHER & I	40	NITA	10
BEA	3	HER MAJESTY	8	OUR LADY OF GRACE	6
BELLE	5	IRENE	4-6	PAMELA	12
BETH	5	JENETTE	10	PANSY	3
BETSY	10	JENNIFER	10	PAT & MIKE	4
BLOSSOM GIRL	7.50	JIM	4-6	PATRICE	8
BLUE BOY	30	JOHN ALDEN	7	PATSY	3
BRIDE	25	JOSEPHINE	9	PEG	4
BRYAN	18	JOY—CHILD	4	PETER	12
BUSTS:		JOYCE	15	PINKIE	25
—BOY(modern)	6	JULIE	6	POLLY	3
—GIRL(modern)	6	JULIET	18	PRISCILLA	6
CAMILLE	8-13	JUNE	3	PRIMA DONNA	35
CAROL	20	KAY	3	PRINCE CHARMING	
CATHERINE	25	LADY DIANA	20	& CINDERELLA	50
CHARLES	18	LANTERN BOY	7.50	PRINCESS	25
CHARMAINE	8-12	LAURA	10	REBECCA	6
CHINESE BOY–GIRL	7.50	LAVON	15	RHETT, PICKET FENCE	7
CHOIR BOYS	3/each	LEADING MAN	35	RHETT, STONE WALL	7
CINDY	10	LILLIAN	6	RICHARD	8
CLARISSA	6-10	LILLIAN RUSSELL	50	ROBERTA	9
CLAUDIA	12	LINDA LOU	12	ROSALIE	17.50
COLLEEN	8	LISA	18	ROSE MARIE, ADULT	20
CYNTHIA	17.50	LORRY YOUNG TEEN	4	ROSE MARIE, CHILD	12
DARLEEN	20	LOUIS XV	35	SALLY, ADULT	5
DAVID	10	LOUIS XVI	28	SARAH	6-10
DEAR RUTH TV LAMP	20-23	LOUISE	6-10	SARAH BERNHARDT	50
DEBORAH	17.50	LYN	4	SCARLET	8-12
DELIA	10	MADAME POMPADOUR	25	SHE -TI	15
DELIA—HAND SHOWING	10	MADONNA CHILD	15	SHEN	7.50
DELORES, YELLOW	13	MADONNA CHILD BUST	12	SHERRI	10
DENISE	20	MARGOT	10	SHIRLEY	10
DIANA	10	MARIE ANTOINETTE	38	STORY HOUR	30
DIANE	10	MARILYN	18	STORY WITH BOY	40
DORA LEE	20	MARSIE	6	SUE	6
DOUGLAS	6	MARTIN	15	SUE ELLEN	8
EDITH—UNUSUAL GREEN	8	MARY SEATED	20	SUSAN	15
EDWARD	15	MASQUERADE	18	SUSANNA	20
ELAINE	4-6	MASTER DAVID	8	SUZETTE	3
ELIZABETH	25	MATILDA	6-12	TESS (TEENAGER)	12
ELLEN	7	MAY	3	VICTOR	13
EMILY	3	MEG	12	VICTORIA	25
ETHEL	7	MELANIE	6-10	VIVIAN	20-25
EUGENIA	20	MEMORIES	25	WENDY	3
EVE	18	MERRY MAIDS:		WYKEN/BLYKEN	3
FAIR LADY	40	—BETTY	3	YULAN	7.50
		—JANE	3	YVONNE	13

CHAPTER 3
A VISIT WITH THE FAMILY

In June of 1994, Clifford Ward, Jr. granted my request for an interview. He graciously offered to allow me time before the interview to photograph several of the pieces of Florence ceramics he and his family still owned. As my sister and I traveled to Southern California, I was not really sure what to expect when I met Mr. Ward, Florence's oldest son. I found Mr. Ward to be a quiet, powerful, and self-assured man in his early 70s. During the course of the interview, I learned he had both fond and bitter memories of the long and tiring hours he spent over the years at the plant to which he and his family gave such a large part of their lives. Mr. Ward was gracious enough to share several of these memories.

Mr. Ward spoke of his mother as an artist with a vast well of talent. The countless pieces in the Florence collection truly exemplify this abundance. In the living room of Mr. Ward's home are several beautiful paintings done by his mother. This is a side of her artistry that few of us will have the opportunity to experience. But this artistic gift does run throughout his family. He described his younger brother as being quite artistic at a very early age, though he died tragically young. Mr. Ward's daughter, Pamela, carries on that tradition. She is an established interior decorator in the Irvine area, near Newport Beach, California. Mr. Ward's son, David, lives in Kennebunk, Maine with his wife and daughter. He, too, has creative talents which he puts into practice as a design and production engineer for point-of-sale display material and bank furniture.

Florence Ward.

Mr. Ward remembers the unhappy times when the designs for the Florence pieces were being pirated by the Lefton Company. The Florence Ceramics Company spent large amounts of money and endured court battles before winning two separate cases of copyright infringement against Lefton. In the end, Lefton circumvented the copyright infringement by slightly altering the Florence designs, moving the placement of an arm or repositioning a hand. Using this approach, Lefton was able to make and import cheap copies of the extraordinary Florence collection.

Mr. Ward recalls a more pleasant memory from the early 1950s, when officials of Royal Doulton China came to visit the Florence Ceramics Company plant. They came to learn from Florence, because in her plant she had developed and used the most modern techniques and general working practices. The Florence Ceramics Company used airbrush overglaze painting for artware and figurines as early as 1951.

Back in those early days, Mr. Ward was the president of the California Art Pottery Association. The magnitude of this is better understood when one realizes that there were over ninety businesses in the association. At the last meeting Mr. Ward attended, in 1991, there were only three firms left.

After the ordeal with the copyright infringement, followed by the death of his father in 1964, Mr. Ward decided it was time to take the family money out of a business which was being challenged by the unsa-

Florence's Rhett appears in white; the Lefton copy of Rhett is in green.

Florence's Delia is trimmed in green; the Lefton copy is smaller.

vory business practices and cheap competition from imports. Before he retired, Mr. Ward worked as a consultant to Scripto, the company which bought the Florence production facility.

Mr. Ward and his children have kept several pieces of the Florence line. I learned from Mr. Ward that his favorite piece of all the Florence collection is The Story Hour, also his mother's favorite. I was delighted by the coincidence—this is my favorite piece, too; it inspires fond memories of the hundreds of bedtime stories read to me by my mother when I was a child.

Mr. Ward was amazed and delighted to learn that there were collectors with four hundred to twelve hundred pieces of his mother's work. I do not think he ever imagined that so many people would continue to collect and cherish the pieces, creating a continual escalation of prices.

Below are photographs of some of the pieces from Mr. Ward's collection.

Mr. Ward is considering leaving his pieces to the Pasadena City Museum in honor of his mother.

Spring Reverie and Companion. 8.5".

Cleopatra and Mark Antony. 12", 13.5"

A pair of Madame Du Barry busts. 8.5"

Leading Man and Prima Donna.

Prince Charming and Cinderella.

Above: Taka (with parasol) and Karlo (with fan). 11".

Left: Portrait. 6"

Right: Rose Marie. 7".

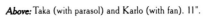

CHAPTER 4
COLLECTORS FROM ACROSS THE COUNTRY

I would like, again, to thank the wonderful people featured in this chapter. Without their knowledge, information, permission to photograph pieces from their collections, and general advice, this book would not exist today. Though I have included several pictures in each collector's section, all of the pictures throughout the entire book are of pieces in one or more of these collections.

Jeannie Fredericks, of Downey, California, has had her collection featured in both *The Encyclopedia of California Pottery* and Harvey Duke's *Official Pottery and Porcelain Guide.* Her first pieces were bought over forty years ago in the Florence Ceramic Company showroom in Pasadena, California; however, she did not begin collecting actively until 1978. She currently has about 350 pieces in her collection. Jeannie's favorite piece is Fair Lady.

Above: Charmaine. 8.5"

Eugenia. 9"

Left: Laura. 7.5"

Delores. 8"

Jennifer. 8"

Grace. 7.75"

16

Yvonne. 8.75"

Joyce. 9"

17

Edith is on the left and Sally is on the right.
7.25" and 6.75"

Shirley. 8"

Sarah is on the left and Ellen is on the right. 7.5" and 7"

Roberta is on the left and Josephine is on the right. 8.50" and 9"

Julie. 7.25"

Ethel is on the left and Jenette is on the right. 7.25" and 7.75"

Mikado. 14"

Patti Smith and her husband, David, of Lakewood, California, did not begin to collect Florence until 1990; however, they did not waste any time building their collection to about 325 pieces. In all of my travels, I have not met any collector with as much exuberance as Patti. Patti's favorite piece is Love Letter. David's favorite piece is Rose Marie, The Child.

Marilyn. 8.25"

Belle is on the left, Peg is in the middle, and Beth is on the right. 8", 7", and 7.5"

Love Letter. 10"

Marianne. 8.75"

Annabel. 8"

Jenette. 7.75"

Marsie. 8"

Young Woman with Blonde Hair and Blue Hat. 9.5"

Delia. 7.25"

Nita. 8"

Colleen. 8"

Cindy. 8"

24

Margot. 8.50"

Patrice. 7.25"

Young Girl in Gold and White with Hand Out. 9.5"

Rosalie. 9.5"

25

Louise and Glen Everett, of Marysville, Washington, have been collecting Florence since 1991. Though Glen is very fond of the Florence pieces, Louise is the avid collector. They have about 685 pieces in their collection. Glen's favorite piece is Prince Charming & Cinderella. Louise is most partial to Fair Lady.

Glen and Louise were kind enough to make a four hour drive to Portland with 100 pieces from their collection. These were pieces which I had not photographed any where else.

Camilie. 9"

Susan/Susann. 8.5"

Madeline. 9"

Cindy. 8"

Sherri. 8"

27

Diane. 8.25"

Barbara. 8.5"

28

Beth. 7.5"

Lisa. 8.25"

29

Colleen. 8"

Grace. 7.75"

Bee. 7.25"

Lavon. 8.50"

Amber. 9.25"

Sally. 6.75"

Nancy. 7"

Martin. 10.5"

Victor. 9.25"

Leading Man. 10.5"

Peter. 9.25"

Jerry and Sue Kline, of Gatlinburg, Tennessee, have about 550 pieces of Florence. Sue's mother got her first two pieces, Yvonne and Gary, in 1951. Sue and Jerry are both collectors and dealers. Because they travel extensively, they were able to purchase a large collection in Florida. Sue and Jerry are extremely knowledgeable about the market for Florence pieces. Jerry's favorite piece is Carmen. Sue's favorite is Grandmother & I.

Patrice. 7.25"

Marsie. 8"

Marilyn. 9.5".

Rosemarie. 8.25".

Jenette. 7.75"

Dora Lee. 9.5"

35

Annette. 8.25"

Lavon. 8.5"

Denise. 10"

36

Carmen. 12.5"

Sally. 6.75"

Darleen. 8.25"

Colleen. 8"

38

Annette. 8.25"

Cynthia. 9.25"

CHAPTER 5
EARLY GARAGE PIECES

When Florence first began to work with clay, she made figurines in her garage. These early garage pieces were mostly children and flower holders. Though they are pleasing, they appear almost crude when compared to her intricate work in the later years. They are much heavier in weight, which is explained by their thicker, bulkier styling.

Young Girl in gold and White, With Hand Out. 9.5"

Rita. 9.5".

Yvonne. 9.5".

Cream and Pink Trim Scarf and Hat. 9.5"

Gibson Girl with Gold Muff. 9.5"

Cream Young Woman with Basket of Red Flowers. 9.5"

Gibson Girl Cream and Gold Flair Dress. 9.5"

Gibson Girl with Dark Hair and Hands Together. 9.5"

42

Young Girl Holding Container. 8.5"

Young Girl In Pink Holding Container. 8.5"

Gibson Girl. 10"

Gibson Girl in White with Gold Trim Holding Bouquet.
10"

Trio of Gibson Girls. 10"

CHAPTER 6
FLORENCE PAIRS

The Florence pairs are figurines which were designed, produced, and sold individually, but with the intention that two pieces would be displayed together as a pair. Some of the better-known pairs are images taken from history, like Antony and Cleopatra, or Marie Antoinette and Louis XVI. Other pairs, such as Cinderella and Prince Charming, Scarlet and Rhett, or Wynken and Blynken, are taken from movies and books. However, many of the adults and children were taken from the artistic imagination of Florence. Some of the best-known groupings in this category are Story Hour and Grandmother & I.

Scarlet and Rhett. 8.75" and 9"

Shen and Yulan. Both 7.5"

Blossom and Lantern Boy. Both 8.25"

Taka (with parasol) and Karlo (with fan). 11".

47

Toy and Ming. Both 9"

Louis XVI and Marie Antoinette. Both 10"

Louis XV and Madame Pompadour. Both 12.5"

Modern Busts. 9.5"

Busts of Pamela and David. 9.50" and 9.75"

Pair of Madonnas. 10.5"

49

Elaine and Jim.. Both 6"

Blue Boy and Pinkie. Both 12"

Douglas and Melanie. 8.5" and 7.5"

Jim and Elaine. Both 6"

Jim and Ann. Both 6"

Madame Pompadour and Louis XV. 12.5"

Leading Man. 10.25"

Lady Diana. 10"

John Alden and Priscilla. 9.25" and 7.25"

Elizabeth and Edward. Elizabeth is 7" wide and 8.5" high.
Edward is 7"

Victor and Musette. 9.25" and 8.75"

Yvonne and Gary. 8.75" and 8.50"

Kiu and She-Ti. 11"

Kiu and She-Ti from the rear. 11"

Martin and Margaret. 10.5" and 9.75"

Reggie and Carol. 7.25".

Don and Judy. 7.25" and 7".

Charles and Eve. 8.75" and 8.5"

Misha and Haru. 11" and 10.5"

56

Cleopatra and Mark Antony. 12" and 13.5"

CHAPTER 7
GODEY DESIGNS

The Godey figurines are taken from the "Godey's Ladies' Book." This was the premier book of American fashion, published during the latter half of the 19th century. It had a vast circulation and, of course, a vast influence. The magazine included many beautiful illustrations as well as articles written on subjects important to women of the day.

Florence used many of the costumes of the Godey period on her pieces. The beauty and elegance made these pieces amongst the most popular of the Florence collection. The amount of detail in these pieces also made them some of the most time-consuming to produce.

Sarah. 7.5"

Scarlet. 8.75"

Ann. 6"

Delores. 8"

Sue Ellen. 8.25"

Genevieve. 8"

Marsie. 8"

Sue. 6"

Sue. 6"

Irene. 6"

60

Kay. 7"

Musette. 8.75"

Amelia. 8.25"

Jennifer. 8"

Georgette. 10.25"

At left, 7.25" tall, Delia by Florence. At right, 7" tall, a Lefton copy of Delia.

Ann, Elaine, and Irene. All 6"

Nita. 8"

Abigail. 8"

Melanie. 7.5"

Camille. 8.5"

Annabel. 8"

Lillian. 7.25"

Jenette. 7.75"

CHAPTER 8
CHILDREN FIGURINES

The death of Florence's youngest son was a painful experience for the entire Ward family. Jack was only sixteen at the time of his death. Florence channeled her grief into making figurines. Many of her early pieces were of children with wonderful smiles in memory of Jack.

It is interesting to note that many of these early children figurines were not given names. You will often find pieces which people refer to rather generically, such as Baby On His Back Holding A Bottle.

These earlier pieces, when compared to her later work, were often less defined and precise. Though they are certainly charming and clearly reveal her love for children, they show less of Florence's artistic talent.

Carol. 7.5".

Linda Lou. 7.75".

Summer. 6.25".

At left, an unknown figure, 7"; at right, Marcella. 7".

Young Girl and Boy with Dog. 6"

Blondie and Sandy. 7.5".

(From left to right) John, Mary, Blondie, and Sandy, all 7.5".

Wynkin. 5.5"

Small Girl with Bird.

Karla, Lisa, and Lisa. 9.75"

Wood Nymph

David, Unknown, Richard. 7.5", 7", 8.5"

Unknown.

Reggie. 7.5".

Rose Marie. 7"

Joy. 6"

(From left to right) Jim, Susie, and Peter. 5.5".

Wynkin and Blynkin. 5.5".

Halloween Child. 4"

Jim and Joyce. 5.5".

David and Carol. 7.5".

David and Betsy. 7.5".

Becky. 5.5".

Small Girl in Pink with Arms Raised.

Peter. 9.25"

74

Fall. 6.5"

Child Ballerina.

Pair of Young Girls in Gold and White.

Pamela. 7.25"

Lisa. 9.75"

Tess. 7.25".

Choir Boys. 6"

76

(From left to right) Jim, Peter, Butch, and Becky, all 5.5".

Lorry. 8"

Pamela and Fall. 7.25", 6.5"

Mike and Pat. 6.25", 6"

Lisa on the left, unknown child in the middle, and Karla on the right. 9.75", 6.75", and 9.75"

Unnamed ballerina. 9"

Linda Lou. 7.75".

Unknown. 6".

CHAPTER 9
FIGURINE FLOWER HOLDERS

In the early years, many of the flower holders Florence made were based on children. In the original catalogues, they were often called "flower containers." Each is made of a figurine, so that it might continue to be displayed in the home even if it is not being used to hold flowers.

Joy and Jerry.

Twin girl and boy. 6.5".

Young Girl in Pink.

May. 6.5"

Patsy. 6"

June. 7"

Emily. 8"

Molly. 6.5"

Wendy.

Bee. 6.25"

Polly. 6"

Sally. 6.75"

Suzette. 7"

Kay. 7"

Unnamed.

Mimi. 6"

Rene.

Ava. 10.5"

Violet on the left, Fern on the right. Both 7"

Gentleman.

Peg. 7"

Chinese Children. 7"

Belle. 8"

Suzette. 7".

From early Garage Era.

(From left to right) Rita, 9.5", and two unknown pieces.

Beth. 7.50"

Baby (flower holder).

Young Boy.

Young Girl.

CHAPTER 10
ARTWARE

The artware classification is quite broad. Generally, it refers to any of the pieces which are not figurines. This includes dishes, lamps, vanity sets, picture frames, birds, animals, and lapel pins.

Vase and Bon Bon dish.

Plain Cornucopia vase on the left, fancy Cornucopia vase on the right.

Dog Ford bank (from the Scripto era).

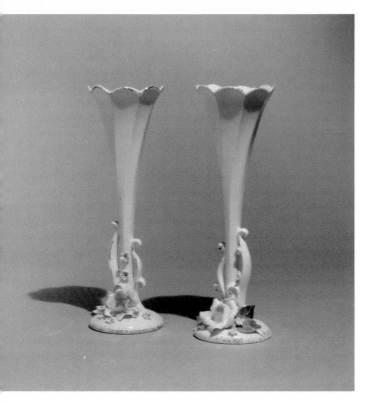

Pair of bud vases.

Shell ashtray.

Fancy Floraline serving dish on the left, and a plain serving dish on the right.

Rose picture frame. 5'" x 7"

Mocking bird.

Cockatoo.

Shell.

Owl.

95

Bookend vases with Peter and Susie.

Gibson Girl lamp.

Diane powder box.

Gibson Girl Lamp.

Pompadour.

A high-buttoned shoe.

A pheasant, with the tail up.

Pouter pigeon.

Angels. 7.75"

A pheasant, with the tail down.

Floraline candle holders.

Floraline sleigh.

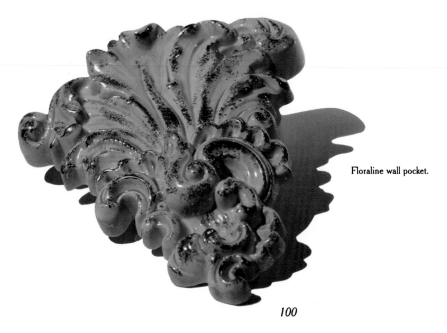

Floraline wall pocket.

100

Cigarette boxes and ashtray.

Cornucopia vase.

Cherub dish.

101

Shell bowl.

Compote dish.

Deep dish bon-bon.

Cottage vase.

Parakeet.

Lapel pins.

Ashtray.

Serving dish.

Floraline basket.

Shell bowl with merry maids: Jane (blonde sitting on top of
bowl), Betty (brunette in bowl), and Rosie (the pair
reclining in front of bowl).

Gibson girl with muff, wall plaque.

Woman with fan, wall plaque.

Woman with purse, wall purse.

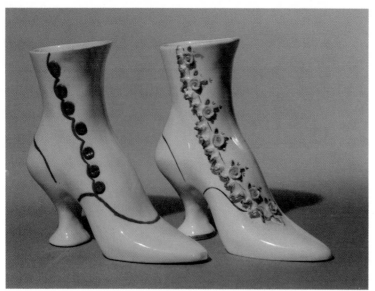

High button shoes.

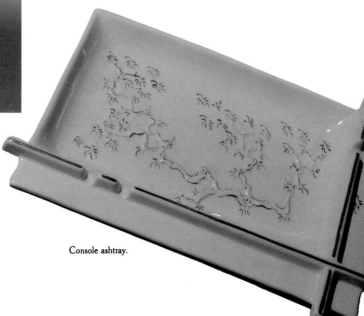

Console ashtray.

Shell wall pocket.

Cameo plaque.

Cameo plaque.

Cameo plaque.

Floraline covered dish.

Lamp.

109

Cornucopia vase.

Our Lady Of Grace.

Madonnas.

Plaques.

Cameo plaques.

Fern flower holder on the left and Violet flower holder on
the right.

Electric mantel clock. 13".

A French electric clock. 11.5".

(From left to right) A shoe, a Florence Ceramic Company sign, and a bon-bon dish.

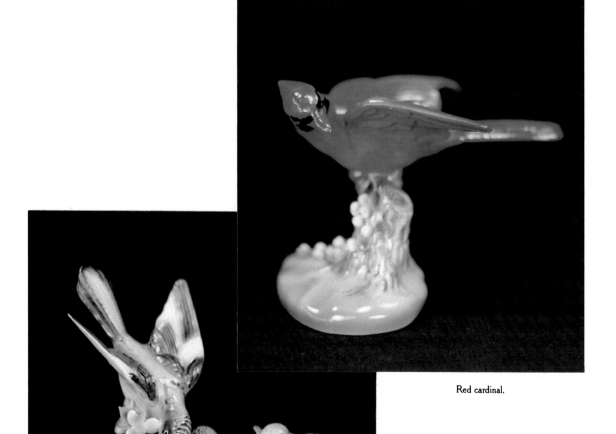

Red cardinal.

Mocking birds.

Bud vase on the left, triple shell dish in the top center, covered box in the front center, and cottage vase on the right.

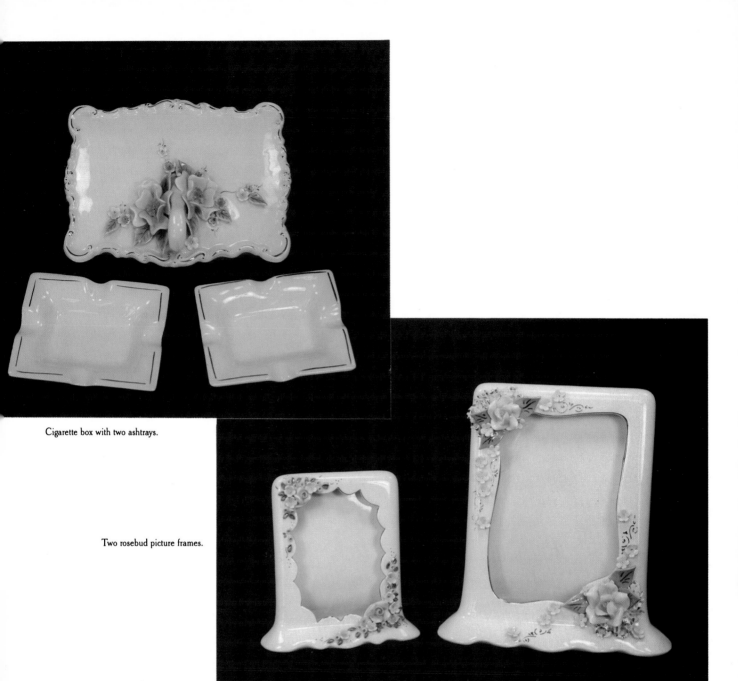

Cigarette box with two ashtrays.

Two rosebud picture frames.

Floraline candle holders.

Baltimore orioles.

Cornucopia vase.

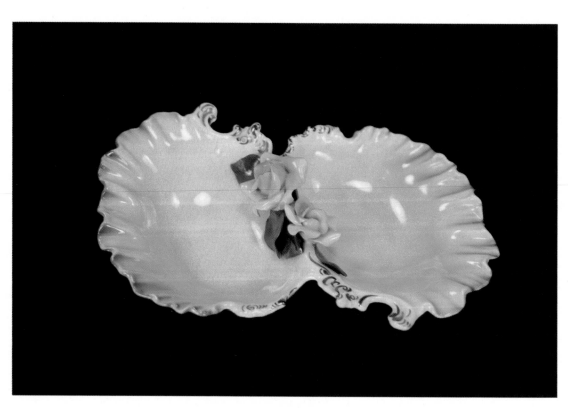

Divided bon-bon dish.

Cigarette box.

Cigarette box.

Swan planter.

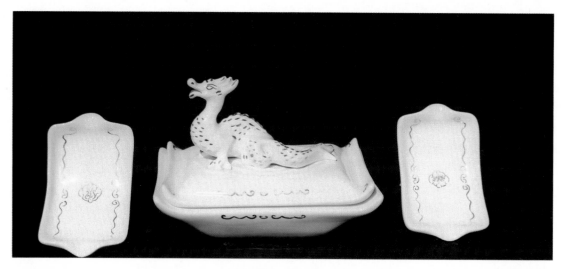

Cigarette box and ashtrays.

Console bowl.

Candle holders.

118

Wall plaque.

Mockingbird.

CHAPTER 11

RARE, UNUSUAL, & HARD-TO-FIND PIECES

The pieces which are classified as rare and unusual are, today, generally found only in collectors' homes, and are rarely found on the market. Some of the better-known pieces in this category are Grandmother & I, which is made as a single piece, Cinderella and Prince Charming, and Mark Antony and Cleopatra.

The rare and unusual pieces are often very elegant, with significant attention paid to the tiniest details. Pieces with details such as articulated fingers or bits of lace often have not survived over the last fifty years without some damage to their exquisite details.

Another example of detail can be found in the two Dear Ruth lamps in Jerry Kline's collection. In these pieces, Ruth is reading a letter. Using the tiniest of gold strokes, actual words were glazed onto the letter, which can be easily read. This attention to detail in and of itself would classify these pieces as rare and unusual. However, there is something else which make them even more unusual. The words in the letters are different on the two Dear Ruth lamps. In the first, the artist wrote "Dear Ruth, I am looking forward to meeting you at the train someday. I love you. MM." The second letter reads "Dear Ruth, I miss you and hope to see you soon." This difference in wording is explained by noting the gold initials (the signature of the artist) are different on these two pieces. The Florence Ceramic Company allowed these personal touches by the artists.

Pieces classified as rare and unusual also include those glazed in uncommon colors or made in very limited numbers. For example, the yellow glaze was quite difficult to produce and was used infrequently. Because so few of the yellow pieces were made, they are zealously sought after by collectors. There also is a "blood red" glaze which was quite unusual. This rare red is of a primary tone, not to be confused with the commonly used, bluer-toned Royal Red glaze. There is also a rare, vibrant green glaze which was used only infrequently.

Also rare and unusual are the figurines wearing actual brocade cloth dresses. Because of the difficulty and cost involved in producing these pieces, very few were ever made. Brocade cloth in the following colors was used: metallic gold with green, vermouth (an off-white similar to the color of white wine), strawberry vermouth, or mint. These figurines often had genuine feathers as hair ornaments. They are marvelous examples of the artistic detailing and authenticity of costuming so much a mark of the Florence Ceramic Company.

Finally, there are some pieces now surfacing which are considered rare and unusual; even the most prominent collectors are seeing them for the first time now. One of these pieces is an unnamed piece known as A Man With A Cart, which may possibly have been designed as a pair with Ava. Another which is also unnamed is known as Baby On His Back Holding A Bottle. One must assume that very few of these figurines were made, or that they have not been traded on public markets.

Fair Lady. 11.5"

Choir boys. 6"

Memories. 5.75" x 6.5"

Edith, unusual in green. 7.25".

Josephine is on the left and Roberta is on the right. 9", 8.5"

Suzanna. 8.75".

Adeline. 9".

Sarah in unusual green. 7.5"

Young girl in matte finish.

Birthday girl. 9"

Florence Ceramics Company dealer sign.

Florence Ceramics Company dealer sign.

Delia with hand showing. 7.25"

Barbara. 7".

Unnamed -basket in textured finish.

Flower holder on the left and figurine on the right.

Bride. 8.75"

An unnamed lamp matching the figures in the above photo.

123

Love letter. 10"

Louise. 7.25"

Sue, in matte finish. 6"

Lillian Russell. 13.25"

Grandmother and I. 9" x 7"

Anna Lisa. 8.25"

Diane powder box. 6" x 6".

Mike and Pat. 6.25", 6"

"Small Fry" Dot and Bud. 7.5".

Meg. 7.75".

Tess. 7.25".

Delores in yellow. 8"

Joy. 6".

Peter. 9/25"

Ava. 10.5"

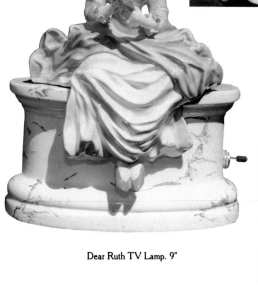

Dear Ruth TV Lamp. 9"

Amelia in brocade. 15"

Man with Cart.

Georgia in brocade. 13.5"

Georgia in brocade from the rear. 13.5"

Lillian Russell in brocade. 15"

Carmen. 12.5"

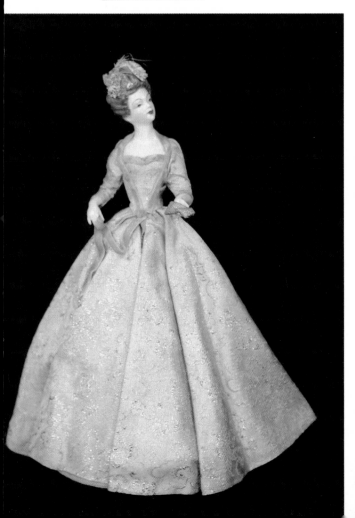

Lapel Pins.

Swan.

Shell bowl with Merry Maids.

Martha.

Lipstick holder.

Baby flower holder.

Powder box, closed.

Powder box, opened.

Deborah. 9.25"

Lorry. 8"

Anita in brocade. 15

Nell Gwen. 10"

Nell Gwen, from the rear. 10"

Cleopatra and Mark Antony. 12", 13.5"

Little Princess powder box.

CHAPTER 12
AN ARRAY OF COLORS

In my travels researching this book, I saw many lovely figurines. I was always impressed by seeing the same figurine glazed in different colored gowns. Some of the colors made the figurine appear far more striking than others. I have chosen just a few of these wonderful comparisons to share with you in this chapter.

Amelia. 8.25"

Vivian. 10"

Vivian. 10"

Vivian. 10"

Matilda. 8.5"

Matilda. 10"

Matilda. 10"

Matilda. 10"

Ava. 10.5"

Matilda. 10"

Ava. 10.5"

Claudia. 8.25"

Claudia. 8.25"

Claudia. 8.25"

Claudia. 8.25"

Her Majesty. 7"

Her Majesty. 7"

Rebecca. 7"

Rebecca. 7"

Elizabeth. 8.5" x 7"

Elizabeth. 8.5" x 7"

Rebecca. 7"

Victoria. 8.5" x 7"

Victoria. 8.5" x 7"

Rebecca. 7"

Victoria. 8.5" x 7"

Chinese Boy and Girl. 7.75"

Chinese Boy and Girl. 7.75"

Catherine. 6.75" x 7.75"

Camille. 8.5"

Chinese Boy and Girl. 7.75"

Charmaine. 8.5"

Abigail. 8"

Camille. 8.5"

Princess. 10.25"

Plain Charmaine on the left and fancy Charmaine on the right. 8.5"

136

Masquerade. 8.25"

Masquerade. 8.25"

Princess. 10.25"

Clarissa. 7.75"

Clarissa. 7.75"

Pamela. 7.25"

Louise. 7.25"

Clarissa. 7.75"

Pamela. 7.25"

Mary. 7.5"

Plain Louise and the left and fancy Louise on the right.
7.25"

Laura. 7.5"

Laura. 7.5"

Carol. 10"

Carol. 10"

Lillian Russell. 13.25"

Lillian Russell. 13.25"

Rose Marie. 9.5"

Rose Marie. 9.5"

Joy. 6"

Joy. 6"

Rose Marie. 9.5"

Joy. 6"

Musette. 8.75"

Musette. 8.75"

Sarah. 7.5"

Sarah. 7.5"

Sarah. 7.5"

PRICE GUIDES

In researching this section of the book, I made a point of contacting many dealers and collectors in every region of the country. I collected data from Massachusetts, Tennessee, Ohio, Indiana, Texas, California, Oregon, and Washington. I believe the prices reflected in this guide are a fair representation of prices across the country; however, this is a guide only and should in no way be considered a definitive valuation of the pieces shown. Furthermore, neither the publisher nor I accept any responsibility for financial losses or gains based on the prices is this guide.

The prices indicate the value of pieces in mint condition; any damage, no matter how slight, will affect the realistic price for a piece. It should also be said that prices do vary according to both the geographic region and the category in which the piece is classified. Rare and unusual pieces are exactly that, rare and unusual. Hence, the prices of these pieces can vary by as much as several hundred dollars, depending upon their availability in a geographic sector.

PRICE GUIDE FOR NAMED FIGURINES

Name of Piece	High $	Low $	Comments
ABIGAIL	Fancy: 175	Plain: 125	Godey
ADELINE	Fancy: 160	Plain: 145	
AMBER	300	250	
AMELIA	800	500	Brocade, Godey
AMELIA	200	100	Godey
ANITA	800	500	Brocade, rare
ANN (YELLOW)	150	125	Godey, rare
ANN (OTHER COLORS)	90	55	Godey
ANNA LISA	125	75	Rare
ANNABELLE	Fancy: 280	Plain: 225	Godey
ANNETTE	200	175	Rare
AVA	175	100	Flower holder, rare
BARBARA	325	200	Rare
BEA	150	100	
BEE	40	35	Flower holder
BELLE	75	70	Flower holder
BETH	90	80	
BETSY	100	90	Youth
BIRTHDAY GIRL	375	350	Rare
BLONDI	180/pair		Paired with Sandy
BLOSSOM GIRL	100	75	Flower holder, paired with Lantern Boy
BLUE BOY	350	300	Paired with PINKIE
BLYNKIN	225	200	Paired
(NOTE: SEE WYNKIN/BLYNKIN)			
BRIDE	400	375	Rare
BRYAN	225	200	Rare, no photo
BUD	350	300	Paired with Dot
BUSTS:			
–BOY (MODERN)	200	150	Matte white
–BOY (TRADITIONAL)	200	150	
–DAVID	200	175	Florence's grandson
–FERN	125	110	Flower holder, paired with VIOLET
–GIRL (MODERN)	200	150	Matte white
–GIRL (TRADITIONAL)	200	150	
–LA PETITE BUST	ND	ND	Rare, no photo
–MADONNA & CHILD	125	100	
–MADAME DU BARRY	150	100	Rare
–PAMELA	125	100	Florence's granddaughter
–POMPADOUR	175	150	
–SHEN	145	125	Flower holder
–VIOLET	125	110	Flower holder, paired with
FERN			
–YULAN	145	125	Flower holder
BUTCH	125	100	
CAMILLE	Fancy: 160-175	Plain: 130-140	Godey
CARMEN	850	700	Rare
CAROL	400	375	Rare
CAROLINE	800	500	Brocade, no photo, rare
CATHERINE	375	350	
CHARLES	200	175	Rare, paired w/EVE
CHARMAINE	Fancy: 150-170	Plain: 100-120	
CHILD BALLERINA	160	150	Rare
CHINESE BOY & GIRL	120	110	Pair
CHOIR BOY	100/piece	80/piece	3 individual pieces
(THE) CHRISTENING	ND	ND	Rare, no photo
CINDY	Fancy: 250	Plain: 100	
CLARISSA	Fancy: 165	Plain: 100	Godey
CLAUDIA (YELLOW)	300	225	Godey
CLAUDIA	125	110	Godey
CLEOPATRA	400	375	Rare
COLLEEN	Fancy: 150	Plain: 125	
COMPANION– SPRING REVELRY	1000/pair	800/pair	Rare
CYNTHIA	300	275	
DARLEEN	275	250	
DAVID	125	100	

Name of Piece	High $	Low $	Comments
DEAR RUTH	500	450	Lamp
DEBORAH	325	300	Rare
DELIA	175	150	Godey
DELIA (HAND SHOWING)	200	150	Rare
DELIA YELLOW	200	180	Rare
DELORES YELLOW	200	180	Rare
DENISE	375	350	
DIANA	200	175	
DIANE	200	175	
DON	175	150	Paired w/JUDY
DORA LEE	ND	ND	Rare
DOT	350	300	Paired w/BUD
DOUGLAS	150	135	
EDITH (UNUSUAL GREEN)	120	110	Rare
EDWARD	250	225	
ELAINE	80	75	Godey
ELIZABETH	375	350	
ELLEN	125	120	
EMILY	40	35	Flower holder
ETHEL	Fancy: 150	Plain: 95	
EUGENIA	260	250	
EVE	150	140	Paired w/ CHARLES
FAIR LADY	850	800	Rare
FALL	90	85	
GARY	170	160	
GENEVIEVE	Fancy: 140-150	Plain: 95-110	
GEORGETTE	290	275	
GEORGIA	800	500	Brocade, rare
GRACE	Fancy: 150	Plain: 100	
GRANDMOTHER & I	700	675	Rare
GROOM	ND	ND	Rare, no photo
HALLOWEEN CHILD	125	110	
HARU	600/pair	575/pair	Paired with MISHA
HER MAJESTY	150	140	
IRENE	60	55	Godey
JENETTE	Fancy: 175	Plain: 110	Godey
JENNIFER	180	175	
JERRY	125	115	Paired w/JOY
JIM	75	60	
JIM (child)	125	100	
JOHN	125	100	
JOHN ALDEN	225	175	Paired with PRISCILLA
JOSEPHINE	250	200	
JOY–CHILD	60	55	
JOY	125	115	Paired w/ JERRY
JOYCE	225	200	
JUDY	175	150	Paired w/DON
JULE	ND	ND	Flower holder, no photo, rare
JULIE	125	120	Flower holder
JULIET	325	300	
JUNE	40	35	Flower holder
KAREN	325	150	No photo
KARLA	200	175	Ballerina
KARLO–FAN	175	150	
KAY	40	35	Flower holder
KIU	250	200	Paired with SHE-TI
LADY DIANA	350	250	
LANTERN BOY	100	75	Flower holder, paired with BLOSSOM GIRL
LAURA	130	120	Rare
LAVON	250	224	Rare
LEA	75	50	Flower holder
LEADING MAN	300	280	
LILA	ND	ND	No photo, rare
LILLIAN	110	100	Godey
LILLIAN RUSSELL	1,000	950	Rare, brocade
LILLIAN RUSSELL	850	800	
LINDA LOU	180	160	
LISA, ballerina	200	175	Rare
LISA	125	110	
LITTLE DON	175	100	No photo
LITTLE PRINCESS	175	150	
LORRY YOUNG TEEN	175	150	
LOUIS XV	300	275	Paired with MADAME POMPADOUR
LOUIS XVI	300	275	Paired with MARIE ANTOINETTE
LOUISE (YELLOW)	175	150	Godey, rare
LOUISE	Fancy: 100	Plain: 80	Godey
LOVE LETTER	300	275	Rare
LYN	75	50	Flower holder
MADAME POMPADOUR	500	400	Paired with Louis XV (ROYAL RED)
MADAME POMPADOUR	500	400	Paired with

Name of Piece	High $	Low $	Comments
MADAME POMPADOUR	400	350	Louis XV (FOREST GREEN) Paired with Louis XV (WHITE)
MADELINE	200	150	
MADONNA	90	80	
MADONNA & CHILD	175	125	
MARCELLA	145	100	
MARDIGRAS	ND	ND	
MARGARET	400	375	Rare, pictured w/MARTIN
MARGOT	200	150	Rare
MARIANNE	300	275	
MARIE	ND	ND	No photo
MARIE ANTOINETTE	450	400	Paired with Louis XVI
MARILYN	300	275	
MARK ANTONY	400	375	Rare
MARLEEN	800	500	Brocade
MARSIE	190	175	
MARTHA	275	200	Rare
MARTIN	190	175	
MARY SEATED	275	250	Rare
MASQUERADE	350	325	Rare
MASTER DAVID	225	200	No photo
MATILDA	150	100	Godey
MAY	40	35	Flower holder
MEG (PINKISH COLOR)	150	125	Rare
MELANIE	Fancy: 125	Plain: 100	Godey
MEMORIES	600	400	Rare
MERRY MAIDS:			
–BETSY	110	75	See SHELL BOWL
–JANE	110	75	See SHELL BOWL
–ROSIE	110	75	See SHELL BOWL
MIKADO	200	150	Paired with TAKA
MIMI	40	35	Flower holder
MING	200	175	Paired with TOY
MISHA	600/pair	575/pair	Paired with HARU
MOLLY	40	35	Flower holder
MUSETTE	Fancy: 200	Plain: 130	
NANCY	Fancy: 135	Plain: 100	
NELL GWEN	500	300	Rare
NITA	150	100	
OUR LADY OF GRACE	175	150	
PAMELA	Fancy: 140	Plain: 80	
PAMELA (WITH BASKET)	125	100	
PANSY	40	35	Flower holder
PAT & MIKE	300/pair	250/pair	Rare
PATRICE	125	100	
PATSY	40	35	Flower holder
PATTY	75	50	Flower holder
PEASANT MAN w/CART	150	100	Rare, (possibly paired with AVA)
PEG	75	50	Flower holder
PETER	250	175	Rare
PINKIE	350	300	Paired with BLUE BOY
POLLY	40	35	Flower holder
PORTRAIT	ND	ND	Rare
POSTER BOY	ND	ND	No photo
PRIMA DONNA	385	250	
PRINCE CHARMING & CINDERELLA	1,000	900	Rare
PRINCESS	450	350	Rare
PRISCILLA	175	150	Paired with JOHN ALDEN
PROM BOY	175	150	Paired with PROM GIRL
PROM GIRL	175	150	Paired with PROM BOY
REBECCA	200	175	Rare
REGGIE	150	125	Paired w/ CAROL
RHETT	175	150	Godey
RICHARD	175	170	Rare
RITA	175	150	
ROBERTA	250	200	
ROSALIE	Fancy: 300	Plain: 275	
ROSE MARIE, ADULT	300	250	Godey
ROSE MARIE, CHILD	150	140	
ROSIE	100	75	No photo
SALLY	40	35	Flower holder
SALLY	125	110	
SANDY	180/pair		Paired w/BLONDI
SARAH	100	75	Godey
SARAH BERNHARDT	600	550	Rare, no photo
SCARLET	Fancy: 200	Plain: 150	Godey
SCARLET (HANDS SHOWING)	325	275	

Name	High	Low	Comments
SHE -TI	250	200	Paired with KIU
SHELL BOWL	100	90	Paired with MERRY MAIDS
SHERRI	200	175	
SHIRLEY	Fancy: 195	Plain: 135	
STEPHEN	350	325	Rare
STORY HOUR	450	400	
STORY WITH BOY	575	450	
SUE	75	50	Godey
SUE ELLEN (YELLOW)	250	200	Godey, rare
SUE ELLEN	125	110	Godey
SUMMER	90	85	
SUSAN/SUSANN (SAME)	300	225	
SUSANNA	300	250	
SUSY	175	150	Rare
SUZETTE	45	40	Flower holder
TAKA WITH FAN	185	150	Paired with Karlo
TESS, TEENAGER	150	125	Rare
TOY	200	175	Rare, paired w/MING
TWIN boy & girl	95	80	As pair
VICTOR	225	200	
VICTORIA	400	350	
VIRGINIA	600	400	Non-brocade, no photo
VIRGINIA	800	500	Brocade, no photo
VIVIAN	250	200	
WENDY	75	50	Flower holder
WOOD NYMPH	175	150	Rare
WYNKIN/BLYNKIN	225	200	Rare
YOUNG GIRL (BISQUE MATTE FINISH)	125	75	Rare, pink tutu
YVONNE	Fancy: 200	Plain: 150	Godey

PRICE GUIDE FOR
UNNAMED PIECES

Name of Piece	High $	Low $	Comments
CHILDREN			
–BALLERINA, SMALL CHILD	145	100	
–BOY & GIRL IN GREEN AND BROWN	125/pr	100/pr	
–BOY WITH DOG	100	75	
–FOUR CHILDREN IN PINK	90/ea	55/ea	
–PAIR OF CHILDREN IN GREEN & WHITE	125/pr	100/pr	
–PAIR OF YOUNG GIRLS IN GOLD AND WHITE	75/ea	50/ea	
–SMALL GIRL HOLDING BIRD	100	75	
–SMALL GIRL IN PINK WITH ARMS RAISED	100	75	
–3 YOUNG BOYS & 1 GIRL IN PINK WITH STRAW FLOWERS	50/ea	30/ea	
–YOUNG GIRL & BOY W/DOG	75/pair	50/pair	
–YOUNG GIRL IN PINK HOLDING BASKET	125	75	basket feels
–YOUNG GIRL WITH PAIL	100	60	
EARLY GARAGE PIECES			
–CREAM & PINK TRIM SCARF & HAT	125	90	
–CREAM YOUNG WOMEN, BASKET OF RED FLOWERS	125	90	
–GIBSON GIRL	125	90	no photo
–GIBSON GIRL CREAM & GOLD FLAIR DRESS	125	90	
–GIBSON GIRL HOLDING BOUQUET	125	75	
–GIBSON GIRL W/DARK HAIR AND HANDS TOGETHER	125	75	
–GIBSON GIRL WITH GOLD MUFF	125	90	
–GOLD & WHITE GIBSON GIRL	125	90	
–TRIO OF GIBSON GIRLS	125/ea	90/ea	
–YOUNG BOY & GIRL WITH FLOWER HOLDERS	100/pr	75/pr	
–YOUNG GIRL WITH BLONDE HAIR AND BLUE HAT	125	75	
–YOUNG GIRL HOLDING CONTAINER	100	75	
–YOUNG GIRL IN GOLD & WHITE, WITH HAND OUT	90	75	
–YOUNG GIRL IN PINK HOLDING CONTAINER	100	75	early garage
FLOWER HOLDERS			
–BABY	100	75	
–CREAM & BLUE WOMAN WITH BASKET & HAT	124	90	
–CREAM & BLUE YOUNG GIRL WITH BOW AND BASKET	125	90	
–MAN IN BLUE & WHITE w/HAT	90	50	
–SMALL BLOND BOY IN BLUE, TRIMMED WITH GOLD	100	75	
–TRIO of EARLY FLOWER HOLDERS	125/ea	90/ea	
–YOUNG BOY IN PALE BROWN WITH DARK BROWN TRIM	75	50	
–YOUNG GIRL IN PINK WITH UNUSUAL HAT	100	75	

PRICE GUIDE FOR
ARTWARE

Name of Piece	High $	Low $	Comments
ANGELS	85	50	
ASHTRAY	35	25	
BABY FLOWER HOLDER	60	50	Unusual
BALTIMORE ORIOLES	225	200	
BLUE ASHTRAY	25	10	
BLUE BOWL	50	25	
BON BON DISH	60	40	
BUD VASE	65	50	
CAMEO PLAQUE	140/ea	90/ea	Set of three
CANDLE HOLDERS	70	60	
CANDY DISH	75	50	
CHERUB DISH	150	125	
CHILDREN BOOKEND VASE	150	125	
CIGARETTE BOXES:	150	125	
–LADIES HEAD ON LID	100	70	
–SCENE ON LID	100	70	
CLOCK - FRENCH - CLC - DRESDEN FLOWERS	550	500	
COCKATOO	225	200	White satin
COMPOTE DISH	75	50	
CONSOLE ASHTRAY	75	50	
CORNUCOPIA VASE	75	50	Pink vase
COTTAGE VASE	90	80	
DEALER SIGNS	350	180	Rare, 3 different
DEEP DISH BON-BON	75	60	
DIANE	250	200	Powder box, rare
DOG FORD BANK	65	50	
FLORALINE BASKET	90	75	
FLORALINE CANDLE HOLDERS	60/pr Pair	25/pr	
FLORALINE CANDY DISH	30	20	
FLORALINE COVERED BOX		40	30 Gold & white
FLORALINE SLEIGH	125	100	
FLORALINE VASE	35	15	
FLORENCE WALL PLAQUE	125/ea	60/ea	Four in set
HIGH BUTTON SHOE	30	20	
LAPEL PINS	150	140	
LIP STICK HOLDERS	300	150	
MOCKING BIRD	125	75	
OWL	225	200	
PARAKEET	150	100	
PHEASANT, tail down	175	150	
PHEASANT, tail up	175	150	
PICTURE FRAMES (5"x7")			
–ROSE–NOSEGAY	130	95	
PINK DISH HANDLES	100	75	
POUTER PIGEON	275	250	
RED CARDINAL	225	200	
SHELL	50	25	
SHELL ASHTRAY	60	50	
SHELL WALL VASE	75	50	
SHOE (BOOT)	55	40	
SWAN PLANTER	300	250	
VOILET/WALL POCKET	65	45	
WALL PLAQUES	140	90	
LAMPS			
–CAMILLE	325	200	
–CHARLES	350	250	
–CLARISSA	325	200	
–CLAUDIA	350	250	
–DEAR RUTH	500	400	TV Lamp
–DELIA	325	200	
–ELIZABETH	350	300	
–GENEVIEVE	300	200	
–GIBSON GIRL WITH HAT	200	175	
–GIBSON GIRL WITH MUFF	200	175	
–LOUIS XVI	500	400	
–MARIE ANTIONETTE	500	400	
–MUSETTE	300	275	
–ORIENTAL GIRL/BOY	325	275	
–SCARLET	300	225	
–VIVIAN	300	225	
–YOUNG WOMAN	200	175	Unnamed, cream & pink
SHADOW BOXES			
–BERNICE (POKE BONNET)	ND	ND	no photo
–JACQUELINE (PILL BOX HAT)	ND	ND	no photo

FIGURINE SIZE & COLOR CHART

Legend

aq = aqua	lv = lavender	sd = sand
be = beige	m = moss green	t = teal
bk = black	p = pink	tr = turquoise
bl = blue	pe = peach	v = violet
g = gold	pr = purple	vr = vermouth
gn = green	r = rose	y = yellow
gr = gray	rr = royal red	iv = ivory
s = strawberry	w&g = white with 22 k gold trim	

Name of Piece	Size	Colors
ABIGAIL	8"	gr&v, aq&v
ADELINE	8.25"	gn, p
AMBER	9.25"	r, aq, m, gr
AMELIA	8.25"	gr, be, bl, gr, gn
AMELIA	15"	Brocade: g&gn, vr, s
ANGELS	7.75"	w
ANN	6"	y, w&g, gr & v, aq & v, be & r, be & gn
ANITA	15"	Brocade: g, gn, vr, s
ANNA LISA	8.25"	w
ANNABEL	8"	rr, t, m, r, v & p
ANNETTE	8.25"	p, t
AVA	10.5"	gr, be
BALLERINA	9"	p, bl
BALLERINA (CHILD)	6.75"	p, bl
BARBARA	8.5"	r, aq, w&g
BEACH KIDS	7.5"	various
BEA (FIGURINE)	7.25"	r, t, w&g
BEE (FLOWER HOLDER)	6.25"	iv&t, iv&p
BELLE	8"	gr, be
BETH	7.50"	gr, be
BETSY	7.25"	p, gn, w&g trim
BIRTHDAY GIRL	9"	p
BLOSSOM GIRL	8.25"	gn, w&g
BLUE BOY	12"	bl
BLYNKEN	5.5"	boy: bl; girl: r
(NOTE: SEE WYNKEN/BLYNKEN)		
BOY WITH DOG	7.5"	w&g
BRIDE	8.75"	w
BRYAN	10.5"	bk, gr
BUSTS:		
—BOY(modern)	9.75"	satin white
—BOY(traditional)	12"	iridescent blue
—GIRL(modern)	9.5"	satin white
—GIRL (traditional)	12"	iridescent blue
—LA PETITE BUST	8.75"	w&g
—MADONNA & CHILD	5.25"	bl with g trim
—MADAME DU BARRY	8.5"	w&g
CAMILLE	8.50"	gr&v, aq&v, be&gn, w&g, m, rr
CARMEN	12.5"	iv, rr with g trim
CAROL	10"	r, v, aq
CAROLINE	6.75", 7.75"	r, v, aq
CATHERINE		Brocade: g, gn, v, s
CHARLES	8.75"	w&g
CHARMAINE	8.50"	gr&v, be&gn, w&g trim on: m, r, t
CHILD BALLERINA	6.75"	bl, p
CHINESE BOY–GIRL	7.75"	w&g, bl & pe, bl & w, gn
CHINESE CHILDREN	7"	multi-colored
CHOIR BOY	6"	bk & w, rr & w, w&g
(THE) CHRISTENING		w&g
CINDY	8"	r, v, aq
CLARISSA	7.75"	gr&v, aq&v, be&gn, w&g trim on: r, rr, t
CLAUDIA	8.25"	shadow pink, green blend, rr
CLEOPATRA	12"	w&g, bl with p trim
COLLEEN	8"	r, t, m
COMPANION– SPRING REVELRY	8.5"	forest gn
COWBOY– COWGIRL CHILD	5"	multi-colored
CYNTHIA	9.25"	r, v, aq
DARLEEN	8.25"	r, m, t
DAVID	7.50"	p, gn, w&g trim
DAVID BUST–FLORENCE'S GRANDSON	9.75"	sd
DEAR RUTH TV LAMP	9"	p, bl, m
DEBORAH	9.25"	r, v, t, m
DELIA	7.25"	rr, r, t, w&g
DELIA (HAND SHOWING)	7.25	rr
DELORES	8"	t, m, y, p
DENISE	10"	r, aq, m
DIANA	6.25"	p, bl, gn, w&g trim
DIANE	8.25"	w&gn, w&p
DORA LEE	9.5"	rr, m, w&g
DOUGLAS	8.25"	gr&v trim, aq&v trim, be&gn trim
EDITH	7.25"	r, w&g, unusual gn
EDWARD	7"	gr on gn, gr on v, w on v, gr on m, gr on t
ELIZABETH	8.25" x 7"	gn on gr, t on gr,v on gr, w on v, r, aq
ELAINE	6"	w&g, gr, w, v, aq&v, be&v, r&g
ELLEN	7"	v with w&g trim
EMILY	8"	iv with w&bl trim, iv with w&p trim
ETHEL	7.25"	aq, r, w&g
EUGENIA	9"	m, r, rr, w&g
EVE	8.50"	r with w&g trim
FAIR LADY	11.50"	r, rr
FALL	6.5"	gn
FERN (FLOWER HOLDER)	7"	w&g
GARY	8.50"	r, rr, t, m, w&g
GENEVIEVE	8"	gr, pr, aq with pr, be with gn trim, w&g, r, t
GEORGETTE	10"	r, rr, m
GEORGIA	13.5"	Brocade: g, gn, vr, s
GEORGETTE	10"	r, rr, m
GRACE	7.75"	r, rr, t
GRANDMOTHER & I	9"x7"	v, w&g
GROOM		bk & w, rare
HALLOWEEN CHILD	4"	multi-colored
HARU	10.5"	rr, w, chinese red
HER MAJESTY	7"	v, w&g
IRENE	6"	w&g with gr&v trim, aq & v, be&v, be&gn, m
JENETTE	7.75"	t, rr, m
JENNIFER	8"	r, v
JIM	6.25"	w&g, gr with v trim, aq with v trim, be with v trim, pe with w trim
JOHN ALDEN	9.25"	gr
JOSEPHINE	9"	m, p, bl, aq
JOY–CHILD	6"	aq, butterscotch
JOYCE	9"	r, v, aq
JULE		unknown, rare
JULIE	7.25"	r with w&g trim
JULIET	8.50"	r, Peacock, w&g
JUNE	7"	w&g
KARLA (BALLERINA)	9.75"	various colors
KAY	7"	iv with bl&w trim, iv with p&w trim
KIU/SHE-TI	11"	pale w with w&g trim
LADY DIANA	10"	rr, v, aq
LADY BUST	7"	w&g
LANTERN BOY	8.25"	gn with w&g trim
LAURA	7.50"	shadow pink, gn, bl, rr, v
LAVON	8.50"	rr, m
LEA	6"	w&g
LEADING MAN	10.25"	r, rr, m
LILLIAN	7.25"	gr, be, w&g, m, bl
LILLIAN RUSSELL	13.25"	r, m
LILLIAN RUSSELL	15"	Brocade: g, gn, v, s
LINDA LOU	7.75"	m, r, t, with w&g trim
LISA	7.25"	r, w&g
LISA (BALLERINA)	9.75"	p
LITTLE DON	5.5"	rr pajamas
LORRY YOUNG TEEN	8"	w&g, gr, lt. p
LOUIS XV	12.50"	velvet gn, rr, w&g, lt. bl
LOUIS XVI	10"	w&g
LOUISE	7.25"	y, gr&v, gr&gn, aq& v trim, be&gn trim, w&g trim on: m, r, t
LOVE LETTER	10"	y
LYN (FLOWER HOLDER)	6"	gr, be
Madame Pompadour	12.50"	velvet gn, rr, w&g, lt. bl
MADELINE	9"	v, m
MADONNA	10.5"	w
MADONNA CHILD	10.5"	pastel bl & g
MADONNA and CHILD BUST	4.75"	pastel bl & g
MARDIGRAS	8.25"	pale gn
MARGARET	9.75"	rr, aq
MARGOT	8.50"	aq, m, rr
MARIANNE	8.75"	r, peacock
MARIE ANTOINETTE	10"	w&g
MARILYN	8.25"	r, v, m
MARK ANTONY	13.5"	w&g
MARLEEN	15"	Brocade: g, gn, v, s
MARSIE	8"	m
MARTHA		r, m
MARTIN	10.50"	m, r, rr. w&g
MARY SEATED	7.50"	w on v, r on gn, v on gr, m on gr
MASQUERADE	8.25"	r, y, aq
MASTER DAVID	8"	r, tr, m
MATILDA	8.50"	gr w v trim, aq with v trim, be with gr trim, w&g, tan with brown trim, m, r, t
MAY	6.5"	w with bl trim, w with p trim
MEG	7.75"	r, t, gn, w&g
MELANIE	7.50"	gr with v trim, gr with gn trim, aq with v trim, ge with gr trim, bl with w&g trim, n, r, t
MEMORIES	5.75" x 6.50"	v with w&g trim, p with w&g trim
MIKADO	14"	rr, w
MIMI (FLOWER HOLDER)	6"	iv with p, iv with bl
MING	9"	w&g, aq
MISHA	11"	chinese red
MOLLY (FLOWER HOLDER)	6.5"	iv with w, iv with bl
MUSETTE	8.75"	rr, r, t, w&g trim
NANCY	7"	m, p, aq
NELL GWEN	10"	m, w&g
NITA	8"	rr, t, m
OUR LADY OF GRACE	9.75"	w&bl&g
PAMELA	7.25"	p with w&g trim
PAMELA BUST– FLORENCE'S GRANDDAUGHTER	9.5"	sd
PANSY	6"	iv with bl&w trim, iv with p&w trim
PAT & MIKE	(Pat) 6", (Mike) 6.25"	aq, y; t
PATRICE	7.25"	r, v, w&g
PATRICIA	7"	lv
PATSY	6"	iv with bl&w trim, iv with p&w trim
PEG	7"	gr, be
PETER	9.25"	r, rr, t, m
PINKIE	12"	p, w
POLLY	6"	iv with bl&w trim, iv with p&w trim
PORTRAIT	8"	r
POSTER BOY		rare
PRISCILLA	7.25"	gr
PRIMA DONNA	10"	r, rr, m
PRINCE CHARMING & CINDERELLA	11.75"	w&g
PRINCESS	10.25"	t, rr, w, w&g
PROM BOY	9.5"	bk & w
PROM GIRL	9"	w&g
REBECCA	7"	gr with v trim, aq with v trim, be with gr trim
RHETT, PICKET FENCE	9"	gr with v trim, aq with v trim, ge with gr trim, gr with gn trim
RHETT, STONE WALL	9"	gr with v trim, aq with v trim, ge with gr trim, gr with gn trim
RICHARD	8.5"	m, r, t, w&g
ROBERTA	8.50"	m, p, bl, r
ROSALIE	9.50"	m, v, with w&g trim
ROSE MARIE (CHILD)	7"	p, bl, w&g, m, r
ROSE MARIE (ADULT)	9.5"	p, bl, w&g, m, r
ROSIE (MERRY MAID)	7"	luster p, bl
SALLY	6.75"	r, w&g
SARAH	7.50"	gr with v trim, aq with v trim, ge with gn trim, bl with w&g trim, m, r, t
SARAH BERNHARDT	13.25"	r, m, w&g
SCARLET	8.75"	gr with gn trim, aq with v trim, be with gr trim, w&g, rr, m, r,t
SHE-TI/KIU	10.25"	w&g trim, lt. bl
SHEN (FLOWER HOLDER)	7.5"	w&g
SHERRI	8"	r, v, aq
SHIRLEY	8"	r, t, m
SMALL GIRL HOLDING BLUE BIRD	5"	iv, p
STEPHEN	8.75"	w&g
STORY HOUR	8" x 6.75"	r, bl
STORY HOUR WITH BOY	8" x 6.75"	r, bl
SUE	6"	w&g, gr with v trim, aq with v trim, ge with v trim, r, t
SUE ELLEN	8.25"	gr with v trim, aq with v trim, be with gr trim, r, t
SUSAN	8.5"	r, v, aq, y
SUSANNA	8.75"	w&g
SUZETTE	7"	peasant girl design
TAKA w/FAN or UMBRELLA	11"	gr
TESS (TEENAGER)	7.25"	p, bl, gr
TOY	9"	w&g, aq
VICTOR	9.25	rr, r, t, w&g
VICTORIA	8.25" x 7"	r on gn, w on v, t on g, v on gr, rr, w&g
VIOLET		m & iv
VIRGINIA	15"	Brocade: g, gn, vr, s
VIVIAN	10"	m, r, w&g, rr, coral
WENDY (FLOWER HOLDER)	6.25"	iv with bl trim, iv with p trim
WOOD NYMPH		p, aq
WYKEN/BLYKEN	5.50"	r, bl
YOUNG GIRL WITH PANTALOONS	4"	w&g
YULAN	7.5"	w&g
YVONNE	8.75"	r, v, t